The Book of
Knots

£3

The RYA Book of
Knots

Peter Owen

Adlard Coles Nautical
London

Published 2001 by Adlard Coles Nautical
an imprint of A&C Black Publishers Ltd
37 Soho Square, London W1D 3QZ
www.acblack.com

Reprinted 2002

First published in the USA by The Lyons Press
under the title *The Book of Sailing Knots*

ISBN 0-7136-5898-3

A CIP catalogue record for this book is
available from the British Library.

Note: While all reasonable care has been
taken in the publication of this book, the
publisher takes no responsibility for the use of
the methods or products described in the book.

A&C Black uses paper produced with elemental
chlorine-free pulp, harvested from managed
sustainable forests.

Typeset in 10/12 pt Concorde Regular
Printed and bound in Great Britain by
The Cromwell Press, Trowbridge, Wiltshire

Contents

Foreword 7

Introduction 9

1 • Rope ends 21
Common Whipping
Palm-and-Needle Whipping
Snaked Whipping
Sealing Ends

2 • Seizings 27
Fat Seizing
Palm-and-Neddle Seizing
Racking Seizing

3 • Splicings 31
Back Splice
Short Splice
Eyc Splice
Eye Splice with Thimble

4 • Stopper knots 37
Overhand Knot
Figure-of-Eight
Multiple Overhand Knot
Heaving Line Knot
Doughnut

5 • Bends 43
Reef Knot
Sheet Bend
Carrick Bend
Rigger's Bend
Surgeon's Knot
Fisherman's Knot
Double Fisherman's Knot
Figure-of-Eight Bend

6 • Loops 53
Figure-of-Eight Loop
Bowline
Running Bowline
Bowline on the Bight
Bowline – Attaching to a Ring
Three-Part Crown
Spanish Bowline

7 • Hitches 63
Half Hitches
Round Turn and Two Half Hitches
Clove Hitch
Constrictor Knot
Transom Knot
Pile Hitch
Anchor Bend

Buntline Hitch
Rolling Hitch
Waggoner's Hitch
Cat's Paw

8 • Decorative knots 77
Lanyard Knot
Monkey's Fist
Turk's Head
Turk's Head – Flat Form
Flat Sennet
Ocean Plait

9 • Net making 89

Glossary 93

Index of knots 95

Foreword

I can vividly remember sail changing incidents when as a novice I clung to the plunging foredeck desperately trying to attach a sheet to the new foresail. As the sail was hoisted I would experience a few nervous moments until it was set and I could be sure that my knot tying had been successful.

We all recognise that the sailing world is becoming ever more technically sophisticated. Despite this, the basic seamanship skills of knot tying and ropework are still vital to the leisure sailor. The RYA Book of Knots is an excellent guide for novice sailors about to attend their first RYA practical course. It's also a useful book for more experienced sailors who want to fill those quiet moments at anchor by extending their repertoire of knots.

Kathryn Burnett
RYA Cruising Manager

Introduction

Sailing has undergone some revolutionary changes in recent years. It is now possible to navigate a craft using satellites and autopilots. Hulls are constructed from a variety of artificial materials, masts are made from aluminium, and rigging on modern-day yachts is almost entirely made of stainless steel. But the one component that has changed very little over time and is still totally necessary for any form of sailing or boating is the knot.

Sailing, like many other pursuits, has seen natural-fibre ropes almost totally replaced by artificial-fibre and wire ropes, but natural-fibre ropes are still favoured by some sailors and have distinct advantages, especially when it comes to decorative knotting.

The RYA Book of Knots gives you the opportunity to master 50 classic sailing knots tied in rope. The knots have been restricted to those tied only in natural and artificial rope to devote each the space for clear instructions and meticulous step-by-step illustrations. Securing rope ends is also fully discussed.

The knots are divided into several distinct groups, each of which is used for different purposes. Practice is essential for good knot tying, so select the right knot for the job and practice until you are confident that you can tie it quickly and securely, in a flat calm or a storm force wind!

History

The art of knotting is as ancient as humankind. Stone Age people used knots to secure and fasten their traps, clothing and housing; coiled and braided rope was found in the tomb of Tutankhamen; the Inca people of Peru used knotted string instead of written figures; and the Greeks, Romans and other civilizations probably knew as much about knots as we do today.

It was, however, seamen and sailors, particularly those who served aboard the great sailing vessels of the eighteenth and nineteenth centuries, who exploited the full potential of knot tying, both practically and decoratively.

The length of the voyages undertaken by sailing ships left sailors with little to do for much of the time; this was particularly true on whalers, which were at sea longer than other ships and were heavily over-manned. Isolated on board, and for the most part unable to read and write, sailors had to find some way to fill their idle hours, and knotting was an ideal way of passing the time.

There was no shortage of raw materials. Sailing ships carried miles of rigging, and there was always a plentiful supply of spoiled rope (known as 'junk') available for knotting. Sailors used their leisure hours to develop ways of tying knots that were both decorative and highly functional.

Knotting on board ship was often competitive, with secrets and intricacies of particular knots jealously guarded. Sailors were also responsible for many of the colourful descriptive names still given to certain sailing knots: the monkey's fist (see page 80) and Turk's head (see page 82), for example.

Ropes

Rope is manufactured in either natural or artificial fibres that can be twisted or braided and is available in a wide variety of sizes. Rope size can be measured by circumference or diameter or by a term; for example, 'twine', identifies a thin line for various uses.

Traditionally, rope was made by twisting fibres of natural materials together. The most commonly used materials were manila, sisal, coir, hemp, flax and cotton. The fibres were twisted first into yarn, then into strands, and finally into rope, in a process called laying up. If you examine a piece of ordinary three-strand rope you will notice the strands go up and to the right, like a corkscrew. It has been 'laid' right-handed. When the rope was made the fibres were twisted together to form right-handed yarn, the yarn was then twisted in the opposite direction to form left-hand strands, and these were twisted to form right-laid rope. If you uncoil one strand you can clearly see it is laid up left-handed, or twisted the opposite way to the whole rope. This is a vital principle of traditional rope making. Even with one strand removed, the other two strands cling together, leaving a groove where the missing strand should be. It is the alternate twisting that creates the tension that holds the rope together and gives it strength.

Three-strand natural-fibre rope

Rope   Strand   Yarn   Fibres

Natural-Fibre Rope

For thousands of years, until shortages during World War II led to the development of man-made fibres, rope was made from natural materials – cotton and flax for manageability, coir and sisal for cheapness, manila and hemp for strength.

Natural-fibre rope is normally three-strand and right-laid. Four-strand, left-laid rope is much more rare and 10 per cent weaker – adding strands does not increase strength. Cable-laid line (a nine-strand cable laid up left-handed from three-strand ropes) is 40 per cent weaker than hawser-laid (three-strand) rope of the same diameter.

Natural fibres are only as long as the plant from which they were derived allows; the ends of these individual fibres, or staples, are what gives natural rope its hairy, rough appearance. This gives them better traction and resistance than smooth man-made fibres. However, natural fibres have many disadvantages: they lack elasticity, and swell and become heavy when wet, making knots difficult to untie; they attract mildew and will rot if not stored properly; they can be weakened and made brittle by strong sunlight, chemicals and salt.

Nowadays, natural-fibre rope is becoming less used in the sailing world, but for decorative purposes many still prefer vegetable fibres for their traditional appearance and the beauty of their natural colours and textures.

Artificial-Fibre Rope

Artificial or synthetic materials have almost completely replaced natural fibres in the manufacture of rope. Man-made filaments can be spun to run the whole length of a line, do not vary in thickness, and do not have to be twisted together to make them cohere. This gives them superior strength.

Braided artificial-fibre rope

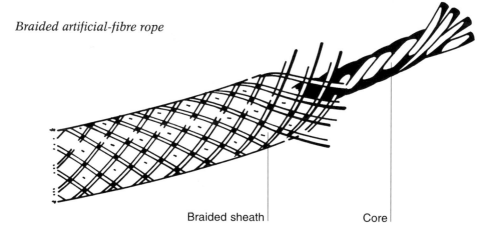

Braided sheath Core

Nylon, first produced in 1938 for domestic use, was the first man-made material to be used in this way. Since then a range of artificial ropes has been developed to meet different purposes, but they all share certain characteristics: size for size they are lighter, stronger and cheaper than their natural counterparts; they do not rot or attract mildew and are not affected by sea-water; they are resistant to sunlight, chemicals, oil, petrol and most common solvents; they absorb less water than natural-fibre ropes, and so their wet breaking strain remains constant; they can also be made in a range of colours. Colour-coded ropes for sailing make for instant recognition of lines of different function. In addition, artificial ropes have high tensile strength, are capable of absorbing

shocks, and have excellent load-bearing qualities.

Nylon (polyamide) fibres make ropes that are both strong and elastic, giving them outstanding capacity for absorbing shock loads. They are good for towing and, because they do not rot or float, they are particularly useful in sailing. One big advantage that sailors have found with this type of rope is that it is far more comfortable to hold and use than natural-fibre rope.

Polyester (Dacron) ropes are nearly as strong as nylon and give very little stretch. They do not float and are highly resistant to wear and weathering. They are widely used in sailing for sheets and halyards. Polyester is also used in small sizes for twine.

Twisted artificial-fibre rope

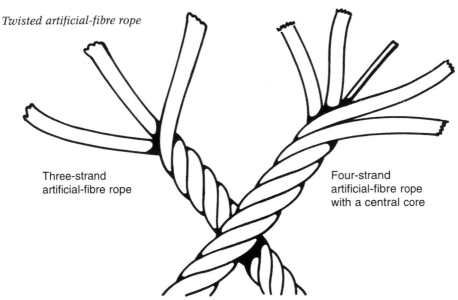

Three-strand
artificial-fibre rope

Four-strand
artificial-fibre rope
with a central core

Polypropylene (polyethylene) is not as strong as nylon or polyester but it does make a good, inexpensive, all-purpose rope. Its one main advantage is that it is the only fibre that floats, thus making it particularly suitable for water-ski tow ropes and rescue lines. Floating does mean, however, that it may be caught in or cut by a propeller.

Because of their very nature, artificial ropes are constantly being developed and improved for a variety of different pursuits. It is always worth checking with your local chandler or specialist rope supplier about any new products that come onto the market for sailing and boating.

Artificial-fibre ropes do have some disadvantages, the main one being that they melt when heated. Even the friction generated when one rope rubs against another may be enough to cause damage, so it is vital to check your ropes regularly. Use plastic tubing to protect sections of artificial rope that you know will be subject to friction. It is also possible for heat friction to fuse knotted rope together so that it is impossible to untie the knot. Another disadvantage is that artificial ropes made of continuous filaments are so smooth that knots slip and come undone. Knots may need to be secured with additional knots or seized.

Artificial rope can be laid up or twisted like natural-fibre rope or it can be formed into braided rope with an outer sheath of 16 or more strands surrounding a central core that is either braided and hollow or made up of solid parallel, or slightly twisted, filaments. Braided rope is softer, more flexible and quite a lot stronger.

Laid-up rope, made of thick multifilaments tightly twisted together, may be very resistant to wear but it may also be difficult to tie, and knots may not hold well. Do not buy a rope that is too stiff. Similarly, be wary of twisted rope that is very soft.

The sheepshank

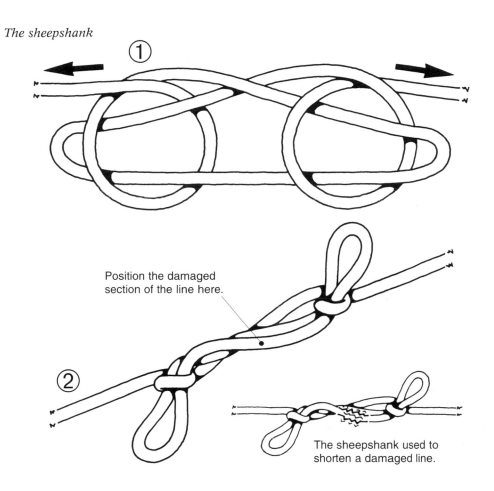

Position the damaged
section of the line here.

The sheepshank used to
shorten a damaged line.

Shortening a Rope or Line

The most successful and secure way
to shorten a rope or line without
cutting it is to use the sheepshank.
The sheepshank is very much a
sailor's knot and shares the special
characteristics of other nautical knots
in that it does not chafe, has a good
jamming action, holds under tension,
and unties easily.

Another important use of the
sheepshank is the emergency repair
of a damaged line. To remove the
strain from the damaged section of
the rope, tie a sheepshank
incorporating the weakened section
in the middle of the knot. This will
provide you with valuable time to
make an effective repair or to replace
the line.

15

Coiling a rope will ensure that it will be immediately to hand and free of tangles when required.

Coil laid rope in a clockwise direction to avoid twisting and kinking.

Looking After Rope

Rope is sturdy material, but it is expensive, so it's worth looking after it properly. Caring for rope will help it keep its strength and prolong its life. Avoid dragging it over rough, sharp edges or dirty, gritty surfaces where particles could get into the rope and damage it. Do not walk on rope or force it into harsh kinks. Inspect it regularly and wash off dirt, grit and oil. Coil rope carefully and always make sure it is dry before coiling, even if it is artificial-fibre rope. If it has been in sea water, rinse thoroughly to remove all salt deposits. At the end of the season, wash all ropes in a mild detergent.

If knots are repeatedly tied in one section of the rope, that section will weaken. The tighter the nip or the sharper the curve the greater the chances that the rope will break; if it does, it will part immediately outside the knot. Finally, never use two ropes of different materials together, because only the more rigid of the two will work under strain.

A cleat

Cleating a Line

A cleat is a deck fitting to which lines are tied on a temporary basis. The line is made fast to the cleat with a hitch. This particular hitch is often the first knot with which prospective sailors come into contact.

It is a simple but effective hitch, and it is also a hitch that many people tie incorrectly. It is easy to think that the more turns you put around a cleat the stronger the connection is going to be. This is not correct. If tied correctly, this hitch only requires a couple of turns to grip firmly and this also then makes it quicker to release.

Because lines have to be alternately made fast and quickly released as a matter of course in sailing, this is an important knot to learn.

Tools

For the majority of sailing knots the only tool that will be required is a sharp implement to cut the rope or line. But the tying of a few knots can be made considerably easier by using some specialized tools. Because certain knot-tying tools are very specialized, they can only be obtained from chandlers or specialist sailing-equipment suppliers.

A selection of the most useful tools and implements are featured here. If you have a particular knot tying problem, contact your local chandler who, in most cases, will be pleased to help you out.

Knife A good quality sharp knife is essential. There are many models on the market to choose from, some particularly designed for sailors. Sharp knives can cause serious injury if mishandled, so always take great care.

Needles Strong needles are used extensively in sailing for repairing sails and ropework, especially whipping and seizing. Special three-sided sailmaker's needles are available, but good strong household needles can be just as effective.

Thimbles These are used to protect rope in an eye splice from chafe (see page 35). They are available in a variety of materials, breaking strengths and sizes.

Mallet A medium-sized wooden or rubber mallet will always be useful on board, but it is particularly useful for working rope into shape or bedding down a splice.

Fid A fid is a sharp wooden spike used to part twisted rope. It is made from hardwood and often has a decorative handle. Great care needs to be taken when using fids because, like knives, they can cause serious injury if mishandled.

Net Needle These are made from wood or, more commonly these days, plastic. Netting twine is wound on to the centre of the needle, which is then used to create a net (see page 89). It is possible to make nets by hand, but to construct a good quality large net a net needle is vital.

How to Use This Book

The diagrams accompanying the descriptions of the knots are intended to be self-explanatory. Written instructions and special tying techniques and methods accompany the more complex knots. There are arrows to show the directions in which you should push or pull the working ends of the rope or line. The dotted lines indicate intermediate positions of the rope. In many of the illustrations lines are shown faded out or cut short for clarity. When tying the knot you should always have a sufficient working end to complete the knot. The amount of working end of rope required can often be calculated by looking at the illustration of the finished knot.

Always follow the numbered order shown when going over or under a length of line; reversing or changing this order could result in a completely different knot, which might well be unstable, unsafe, and insecure.

Parts of the Rope

KNOT

WORKING END

STANDING PART

BIGHT

1

Rope Ends

A slowly unravelling rope with frayed
ends is annoying, wasteful and, in
some cases, dangerous. But a rope
with correctly sealed ends is safe,
neat and makes knots significantly
easier to tie.

Artificial-fibre ropes are now
widely used in sailing and have many
advantages, one of them being that
the rope ends can be quickly and
efficiently heat sealed to prevent
them from fraying. But natural-fibre
ropes are still used and, if left
unseized, the ends will fray. A secure
and easy way to prevent this is by
whipping the ends. Use vegetable-
fibre twine or waxed-polyester twine
and always bind against the lay.

Common Whipping

This easily tied and practical whipping is, as its name suggests, one of the most widely used forms of whipping. But it should be remembered that if the rope end frequently becomes wet, most whipping twines will swell and stretch. This can lead to the whipping loosening and slipping off. So for rope ends that are subject to becoming wet, this should be seen as only a temporary whipping.

Trim the loose ends of the whipping twine and make neat the rope strand ends. With artificial ropes, the strand ends can be heat sealed.

Palm-and-Needle Whipping

This durable and reliable whipping is especially suited to twisted natural-fibre rope, but can also be tied on braided or artificial-fibre ropes. It will stand up well to friction, so it can be employed for heavy usage. You will need a needle with an eye big enough to take whipping twine. Special sailmaker's needles are available for this purpose.

To ensure the knotted end of the twine is held securely, push the needle through the centre of a strand.

Make the required number of turns toward the rope end and then push the needle behind one of the rope strands.

Follow the gap between the strands down to the lower end of the whipping. Insert the needle so that it exits from the next gap and follow back to the top of the whipping. Continue to create this diagonal line running down each gap.

To finish, pull the twine under the whipping and trim the loose ends. If the rope is braided rather than twisted, the diagonal lines can still be added.

23

Snaked Whipping

This decorative and highly effective whipping is more suited to large-diameter ropes; it can prove difficult to tie on thinner ropes. It is important with all whipping, and especially snaked whipping, to make sure that each turn is pulled as tight as possible. Also, to make the snaking less likely to slip, as you pass the needle under the whipping, pick up a few fibres of the rope itself. The decorative appearance of this whipping makes it ideal for ropes that are left out on show or on board.

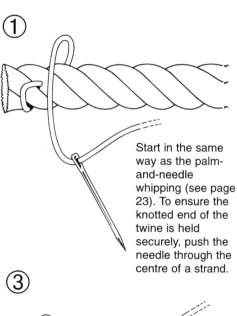

Start in the same way as the palm-and-needle whipping (see page 23). To ensure the knotted end of the twine is held securely, push the needle through the centre of a strand.

Make the required number of turns away from the rope end and then push the needle through the rope, keeping the turns tight.

Create the snaked pattern using the two end strands of the whipping to secure the diagonal crosses.

To finish, knot the twine with two half hitches, push the hitches under the whipping, and trim the loose ends.

Sealing Ends

Apart from whipping the ends of rope, there are three other options to consider for sealing ends.

All synthetic-rope ends can be sealed using heat. When you buy synthetic rope from a chandler they will cut it to the required length using an electrically heated knife, which gives a neat, sharp edge.

When you cut synthetic rope yourself, use a sharp knife and then melt the end with a cigarette lighter, match or on an electric/gas ring.

A quick and efficient method for creating a temporary seal is to use ordinary adhesive or electrical tape. And, finally, on small stuff (any rope which has a circumference of less than 1in), a simple stopper knot will provide an effective seal.

Heat sealed synthetic rope

Rope sealed with adhesive or insulating tape

Rope sealed with a stopper knot

2

Seizings

A seizing is used to bind two ropes together. The same thickness and type of twine or small stuff used for whipping is generally used for seizing.

Seizing can be used to bind two separate parts of rope together but it is most widely used to bind the same piece of rope together to form an eye.

Flat Seizing

This simple form of seizing is good for light loads and to temporarily bind two pieces of rope together. For this type of seizing, use twine or thin line that has been prepared with a small eye at one end.

Prepare the seizing twine by forming a small eye in one end. This is done by opening up the strands and tucking the twine end through a couple of times.

(1) Start by making a series of tight turns around the two ropes

(2) When sufficient turns have been made, thread the twine down between the two ropes and make a series of turns around the seizing at 90° to the original turns.

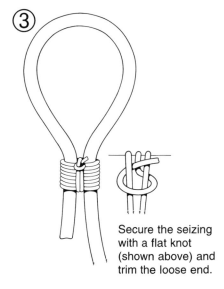

(3) Secure the seizing with a flat knot (shown above) and trim the loose end.

Palm-and-Needle Seizing

This method of seizing creates a strong grip on the rope, making it suitable for heavy loads. It is particularly useful for making eyes in the end of ropes. It is recommended that you use a sailmaker's needle to thread the twine through the rope.

Knot the end of the twine and thread it through one of the ropes. Take the twine up to the point at which the seizing will finish and insert the needle back through the rope, across and out of the other rope.

Return to the start point and insert the needle through the second rope. Pull the twine tight, continue, and finish in exactly the same way as flat seizing (see previous page).

Racking Seizing

This form of seizing should be used if the seized rope parts are to be subject to excessive, uneven or sideways loading. Instead of making complete turns, thread the twine over and under the ropes. This will substantially strengthen the seizing. Racking can be applied to flat seizing (see page 28) and palm-and-needle seizing (see page 29).

Thread the twine over and under the rope.

3

Splicings

Splicing is a method of joining rope to itself or to other rope by interweaving the separate strands. It is a very reliable technique and one that every sailor should know.

If you encounter difficulty in separating rope strands, use a fid (see page 19). Most ropework, and especially splicing, benefits from being worked into shape and this can be done by being rolled underfoot or by using a wooden mallet or rubber-faced hammer. All the examples covered in this chapter are illustrated with the most commonly used three-stranded rope.

Back Splice

This is one of the most widely used splices in the sailing world. It is also known as Spanish whipping.

It creates a decorative and practical end to a rope and, unlike whipping, it becomes firmer and stronger with time.

The crown knot

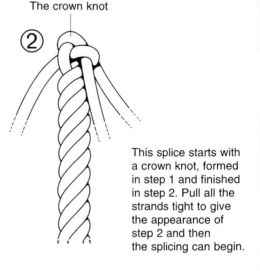

This splice starts with a crown knot, formed in step 1 and finished in step 2. Pull all the strands tight to give the appearance of step 2 and then the splicing can begin.

Take a strand and lead it against the lay of the rope over the next strand, and under the third strand.

Continue to do the same with the other two strands, making sure the strands leave the knot at regular intervals of 120°. To complete, work against the lay, take each loose strand in turn over the strand directly beneath it, and tuck underneath the next strand. Tuck each strand two or three times, keeping the splice as tight as possible. Trim the strand ends, being careful not to trim them too close, as this could lead to the splice unravelling.

Short Splice

This splice provides the ideal solution for permanently joining the ends of two ropes with little loss of strength. It can also be successfully used to repair a break in a line.

① Unlay the end of each rope and bring them together so that each strand of one lies between each strand of the other.

② Temporarily tie the loose strands of one rope along the other.

③ Take one of the loose strands over one strand and under the next.

④ Repeat the over-one-under-one tuck with the second and third strand and then repeat the whole process, tucking each strand two or three times.

⑤ To complete, turn the assembly around, remove the temporary fixing, and tuck exactly the same as for the first half. Trim the loose ends, then place the splice on the floor and roll it under your shoe to make it uniformly round.

Eye Splice

This is one of the most important sailing knots and one that every sailor should learn. You will always need eyes in the end of your ropes and the eye splice is the most reliable way of achieving this.

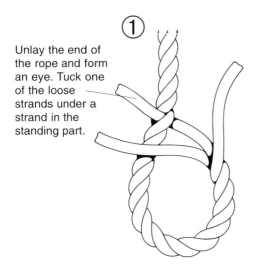

Unlay the end of the rope and form an eye. Tuck one of the loose strands under a strand in the standing part.

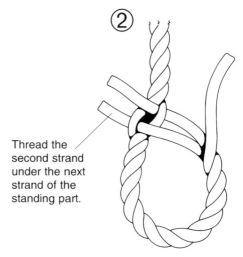

Thread the second strand under the next strand of the standing part.

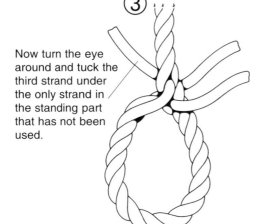

Now turn the eye around and tuck the third strand under the only strand in the standing part that has not been used.

To complete, repeat the process putting in two more tucks for each strand, making sure the splice is kept as tight as possible. Trim the loose ends and roll the splice between your hands to make it uniformly round.

Eye Splice with Thimble

If subject to heavy use and chafing,
an eye splice can be reinforced and
strengthened with a thimble.
Thimbles are made from various
metals or plastic and are available in
a wide variety of sizes. The splice can
be either tied around or stretched
over a thimble.

Whipping that is kept
well away from the
working surface will
secure a loose
thimble.

Thimble

4

Stopper Knots

Stopper knots, as their name suggests, are used to prevent the end of a rope or line slipping through an eye, loop or hole. They can be used to bind the end of a line so that it will not unravel and can also be used decoratively. At sea they are used to weight lines and at the ends of running rigging.

The most important knot of this type is the overhand. This is the simplest, and perhaps the oldest, knot known to man and is used as a basis for countless others.

Overhand Knot

Also known as the thumb knot, this knot forms the basis for many others. It is used in its own right as a stopper knot and is tied at regular intervals along lines to make them easy to grip. If a line develops an unwanted overhand knot, undo it immediately, as this knot is very difficult to untie, especially when the rope is wet.

To make a line easy to grip, tie the overhand knot at regular intervals along the line.

Figure-of-Eight

The knot's name comes from its characteristic shape. It is the most important stopper knot for sailors, used on running rigging. (It is also known as the Flemish knot or the Savoy knot).

The knot is made in the end of the line, with the upper loop around the standing part and the lower loop around the working end. When tying this knot you should leave a tail on the working end. This will enable you to grasp the knot should it become jammed.

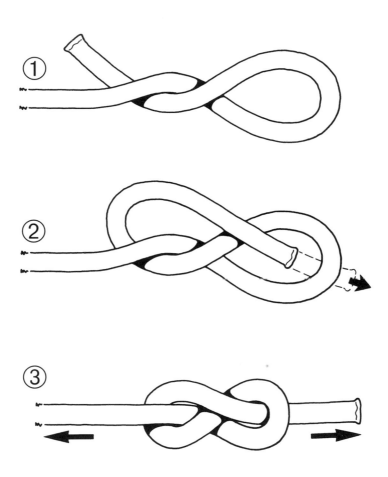

Multiple Overhand Knot

This knot, also known as the blood knot, earned its other name because it was the knot used to weight the ends of the lashes in the cat-o'-nine-tails, the whip historically used to flog soldiers, sailors and criminals. Its main sailing uses are as a weighting or stopper knot made with a small-diameter line.

When tying the knot, keep the loop open and slack as you make the turns and gently pull on both ends at the same time, twisting the two ends in opposite directions. Like many stopper knots, this knot is difficult to untie when the line is wet.

Heaving Line Knot (or Stopper Knot)

When a heavy line is thrown from boat to shore or to another vessel, a heaving line knot is used. The heavy line is attached to a heaving line, a lighter line that is thrown across the gap first so that the heavier line can be drawn behind it. The heaving line knot is tied in the end of this lighter line to give it weight and aid in throwing. Heaving lines are usually $\frac{1}{2}-\frac{3}{4}$ in, in diameter and may be up to 80ft long. They should float, be flexible, and be strong enough to bear a man's weight.

Doughnut

This decorative heaving line knot has the obvious advantage that other lines can be easily tied to it or it can be hooked on or over objects. The weight of this knot can be increased by wrapping a narrow strip of sheet lead around the original three coils before making the final turns. The doughnut also has a very useful secondary use: when it is tied in small material without the sheet lead, it can be used at the end of any cord that you need to pull.

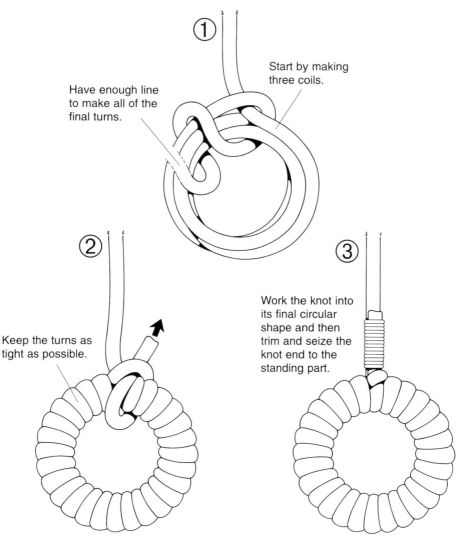

① Start by making three coils.

Have enough line to make all of the final turns.

② Keep the turns as tight as possible.

③ Work the knot into its final circular shape and then trim and seize the knot end to the standing part.

5

Bends

Bends are used to join two lengths of rope at their ends to form one longer piece. It is important, if bends are to be secure, for the ropes joined in this way to be of the same kind and the same diameter. The sheet bend (see page 45) is the exception to this rule. It is secure, even when it is used to join ropes of different diameters.

Bends used at sea can often be made totally secure and more streamlined by seizing any loose ends.

Reef Knot

The reef knot gets its name from its nautical use to tie two ends of a rope when reefing a sail. It is often the only knot many people know – apart from the granny knot.

The reef knot is not a secure bend and should not be used as one, certainly never with ropes of different diameters. Its true function is to join together the ends of the same rope or string. It should *only* be used to make a temporary join in lines of identical type, weight and diameter, where it will not be put under great strain. If the lines have to take strain, stopper knots should be tied in the short ends.

The knot is made up of two half knots. The first half knot starts left over right, the second is added right over left, and both short ends finish on the same side. A correctly tied reef knot is symmetrical. If the knot is raised and uneven, it is a granny knot, which is not secure and should be avoided.

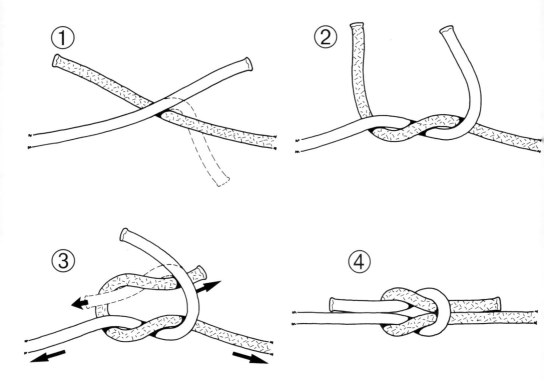

Sheet Bend

The sheet bend is probably the most commonly used of all bends and, unlike most other bends, it can safely join lines of different thickness. It is not, however, 100 per cent secure, especially with synthetic rope, and should never be used in circumstances where it will be subjected to great strain. Its breaking strength also decreases in direct proportion to the difference of the lines joined.

The sheet bend derives its name from the way the knot was originally used on sailing ships to secure the trimming ropes (known as sheets) to sails. When put to its other traditional use, as the knot used to join the corners of a flag to the halyard when it is hoisted and lowered, it is known as the flag bend. It is quick to make and easy to untie, by rolling forward the bight that encircles the single line, and is one of the basic knots that all sailors should know.

A slipped sheet bend is formed by placing a bight between the loop of the heavier rope and the standing part of the lighter one. The slipped knot is easiest to untie when the rope is under strain.

The slipped sheet bend

45

Carrick Bend

Its name probably derives from a medieval Western European ship, the carrack. The knot is formed from two overhand knots crossing each other. It is a very stable knot, does not slip, and is one of the most secure ways of joining two ropes of similar diameter but different type. It is rarely used as a temporary knot as it is very hard to undo when wet or if it has been subjected to very heavy strain. It can be used with larger-diameter ropes such as hawsers, tow lines and mooring lines.

In its flat form it is valued for its distinctive symmetric appearance and has long been a favourite among artists and graphic designers. When it is drawn up it capsizes into an entirely different shape, but this has no detrimental effect on its strength or security.

Rigger's Bend

The rigger's bend or Hunter's bend is based on two overhand knots. It is stable, has good grip, and is stronger than the sheet bend or the reef knot. It also has the advantage of being easy to untie.

The name Hunter's bend came from Dr Edward Hunter, a retired physician, who was reported to have invented the knot in 1968.

Subsequent research, however, revealed his knot to be the same as the rigger's bend described nearly 20 years earlier by Phil D Smith in an American book called *Knots for Mountaineers*. He had devised the knot while working on the waterfront in San Francisco. Whoever first invented it, the rigger's bend or the Hunter's bend remains a good general-purpose sailing knot with many useful qualities.

Surgeon's Knot

This knot, as the name suggests, is used by surgeons to suture wounds and tie off blood vessels. It is also an excellent sailing knot for joining two lengths of rope or line together. It is less bulky than other knots and has a good grip. It twists as it is drawn up tight and the diagonal is wrapped around it.

Fisherman's Knot

This knot is said to have been invented in the nineteenth century, but some authorities suggest it was known to the ancient Greeks. It is generally known as the fisherman's knot, but over the years it has picked up many different names (such as the angler's knot, English knot, Englishman's bend, halibut knot, true lover's knot and waterman's knot). It is formed from two overhand knots that jam against each other; the short ends are on opposite sides and lie almost parallel to their nearest standing part. After use, the two component knots are generally easily separated and undone.

The fisherman's knot is best suited to joining thin lines such as string, cord, twine or small stuff, and, as the name suggests, it is widely used by fishermen for joining the finest of fishing lines.

Seize the ends to streamline the knot.

Double Fisherman's Knot

This double version of the fisherman's knot is a very strong knot for joining thin lines. It is also known as the grapevine knot. It is quite a bulky knot, so often the ends are seized to streamline the knot and prevent it from catching.

Seize the ends to streamline the knot.

Figure-of-Eight Bend

This simple knot (also known as the Flemish bend or knot) is tied by making a figure-of-eight knot in one end of a line and then following it around with the other working end. It is, despite its simplicity, one of the strongest bends and holds equally well in string and rope.

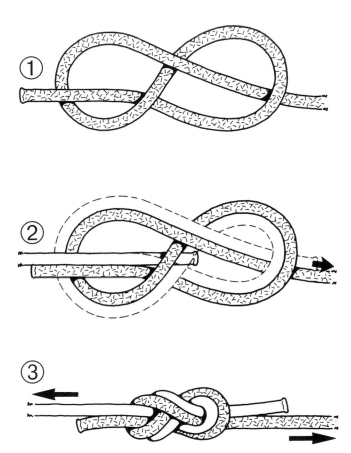

6

Loops

Knots made in the end of a rope by
folding it back into an eye or loop
and then tying it to its own standing
part are called loops. Unlike hitches,
which are formed around an object
and follow its shape, loops are made
in the hand, generally to drop over
an object.

Loops are the most commonly
used group of sailing knots, and are
particularly important to sailors.

Figure-of-Eight Loop

This knot is relatively easy to tie and stays tied, even when stiff rope is used. It has many sailing applications, especially when a quick, but strong, eye or loop is required at the end of a rope. Its disadvantages – it is difficult to adjust and cannot easily be untied after loading – tend to be outweighed by its usefulness. It is also known as the 'figure-of-eight on the bight'.

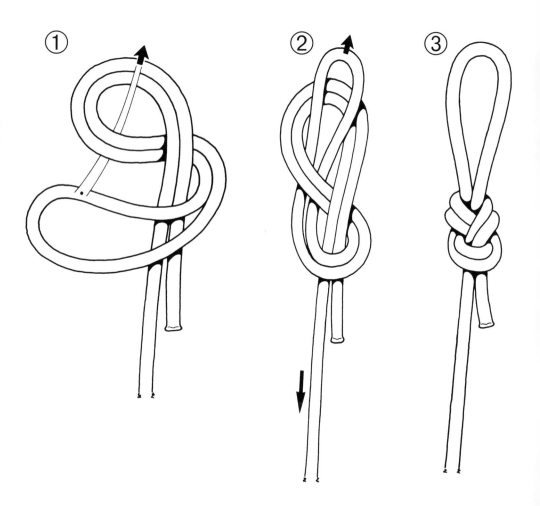

Bowline

The bowline is one of the best known and widely used knots and is particularly important to sailors. It is tied to form a fixed loop at the end of a line or to attach a rope to an object. It has many sailing applications, including use on running rigging and for hoisting, joining and salvage work.

The bowline is simple to tie, strong and stable. Its main advantages are that it does not slip or come loose, even in polypropylene ropes that allow other knots to slip. It is also quick and easy to untie, even when the line is under tension, by pushing forward the bight that encircles the standing part of the line.

For extra security, finish off the bowline with a stopper knot or an extra half hitch – but remember that this may well not be easy to untie.

Additional stopper knot

Running Bowline

This is probably the only running knot used by sailors; it is used on running rigging and to retrieve floating objects that have fallen overboard. On old sailing ships this knot was used in strong winds to tighten the square-sail to the yard-arm.

The running bowline has many uses because it is strong and secure, does not weaken rope, is simple to untie and slides easily. It is useful for hanging objects with ropes of unequal diameters – the weight of the object creates the tension that makes the knot grip.

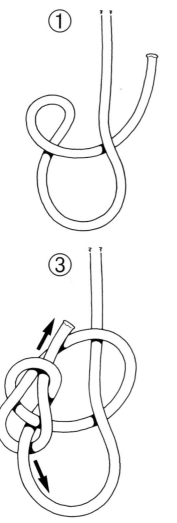

Bowline on the Bight

The bowline on the bight forms two fixed loops that do not slide. They are of the same diameter and overlap each other but, when opened out, they can be used separately. Although an ancient knot, it is still used today – especially in sea rescues. If the person to be rescued is conscious, he or she puts a leg through each loop and holds on to the standing part. If the person is unconscious, both legs are put through one loop and the other loop goes under the armpits. This knot is equally effective in salvaging objects.

Bowline – Attaching to a Ring

This variation for tying the bowline is particularly useful for attaching boats to rings. The standing part stays taut throughout while the working end is used to tie a secure fastening.

Three-Part Crown

This sturdy, secure, double-loop knot can be used as a decorative knot from which to hang gear or equipment, on board ship or on shore.

Spanish Bowline

This is a very strong knot that is widely used in rescue work at sea. The Spanish bowline can also be used to hoist large objects in a horizontal position.

Like the bowline on a bight (see page 57), it is a very old knot, formed of two separate and independent loops that will hold securely and are very safe, even under considerable strain. To effect a rescue, one loop is slipped over the casualty's head, around the back and under the armpits; the other loop goes around the legs behind the knees. It is vitally important that each loop is tightened to the individual's size and then locked into position. If this is not done properly, an unconscious person could easily fall through the loops.

7

Hitches

Hitches are knots used to secure a rope to another object (such as a post, hook, spar or rail) or to another rope that does not play any part in the actual tying.

They are widely used in sailing for mooring boats, fastening lines and lashing. They can stand parallel strain without slipping and have the advantage of being very quick to tie.

Half Hitches

The half hitch is a very widely used fastening. It is, in fact, a single hitch formed around the standing part of another hitch. It is used to complete and strengthen other knots – as in the 'round turn and two half hitches' (see opposite page) – which can then be used for tying, hanging, hooking objects, etc. The slipped half hitch is a useful variation of the simple half hitch; a sharp pull on the end releases the knot.

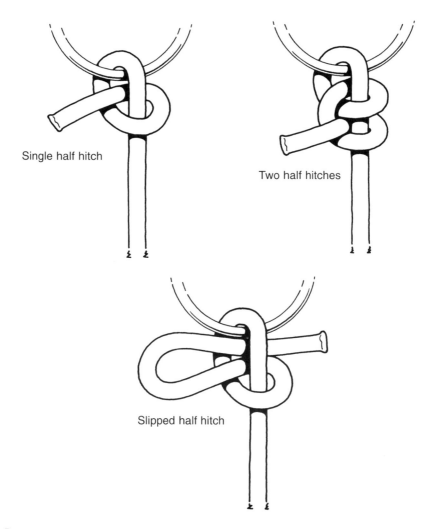

Single half hitch

Two half hitches

Slipped half hitch

Round Turn and Two Half Hitches

This knot is strong, dependable and never jams. This makes it a very versatile sailing knot; you can use it whenever you want to fasten a line to a ring, post, bollard, deck eye, rail or beam. It moors boats safely and will support heavy loads. It has another advantage in that once one end has been secured with a round turn and two half hitches, the other end can be tied with a second knot. This is especially useful when fastening unwieldy, bulky objects.

Clove Hitch

The clove hitch is one of the best known and most valuable of hitches and is used extensively on most yachts. It can be used to fasten a line to a rail, post or bollard, or on to another rope that is not part of the knot. It can, with practice, be tied with one hand. As one of its other names, the boatman's knot, suggests, it is particularly useful for sailors who may need to moor a dinghy to a dock with one hand while holding on to a rail with the other.

The clove hitch is not, however, a totally secure mooring knot, as it will work loose if the strain is intermittent and comes from different angles. It is best used as a temporary hold, and then replaced by a more stable knot. It can be made more secure by making one or two half hitches around the standing part of the rope, or by adding a stopper knot.

A useful alternative method of constructing a clove hitch is to form the knot before dropping it over a post or bollard.

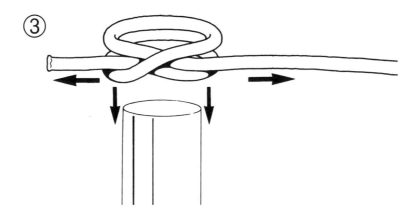

Constrictor Knot

This is a popular all-purpose knot because it is firm and does not slip. It is particularly useful for creating a quick temporary whipping on the ends of ropes.

The knot is made by taking two turns with the rope, forming an overhand knot in the second. The left end is then threaded under the first turn, trapping the overhand knot

(see page 38) under a crosswise turn that holds it firmly in place. The constrictor knot grips firmly and stays tied. It may have to be cut free unless the last tuck is made with a bight to make a slip knot.

An alternative way of tying this knot is to follow steps 1 and 2 of the clove hitch, but before finishing pass the working end over and under the first turn.

Transom Knot

This is similar to a constrictor knot (see previous page). It is used to fix together crossed pieces of rigid material and has a wide range of sailing uses; for example, to secure paddles to luggage racks. If used as a permanent knot, the ends may be trimmed off for neatness.

Pile Hitch

The pile hitch is a very neat and practical hitch for securing objects to a post. It is ideal for the temporary mooring of a boat. The big advantage of this hitch is that it is very easy to tie quickly.

Anchor Bend (or Fisherman's Bend)

The anchor bend, also known as the fisherman's bend, is one of the most secure and widely used sailing hitches. It is formed by making two turns around a post or through a ring and then tucking the working end through both turns.

An additional stopper knot or half hitch can be used for added safety, but if the anchor bend is to be used as a long-term fixing (for example, to tie onto an anchor ring), the working end should be secured with a seizing for total security.

Additional
half hitch

Buntline Hitch

This hitch is specifically used for attaching buntlines to the eyes or eyelet holes in sails. The buntline hitch needs to be very secure so as to avoid loosening in strong winds that constantly buffet sails. Its strength comes from the short end being deliberately trapped inside the knot.

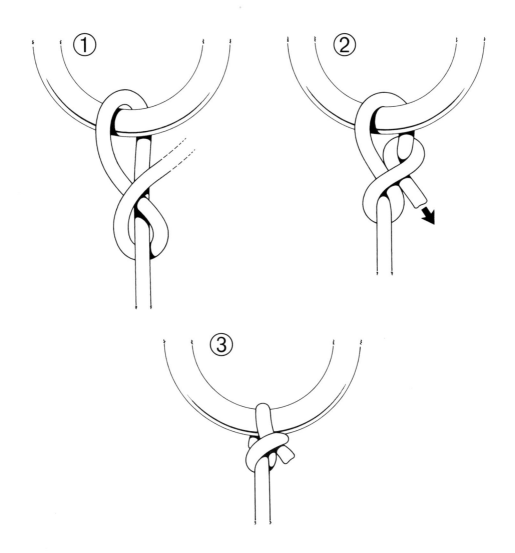

Rolling Hitch

This is an essential knot for windsurfers. It is derived from the clove hitch but is significantly more secure. It is used on windsurfers to secure the wishbone boom to the mast, but can be used equally well to make any line fast to other cylindrical objects. This very effective, reliable knot is easy to tie and it grips itself, but only in one direction.

The knot will grip when pulled in the direction of the standing part.

Waggoner's Hitch

The waggoner's hitch is a very useful, practical knot that allows a line or rope to be pulled tight yet ready for immediate release. This makes it an ideal knot for securing loads or deck gear. Once the line has been heaved tight, it should be secured with at least two half hitches.

Cat's Paw

This is the best hook knot for rope of medium diameter because the strain is equal on both sides. It has a long history of use on the docks and at sea for lifting and slinging heavy loads. This very secure knot can be used, for example, on the hook of a crane in the marina.

8

Decorative Knots

Decorative knots can be used individually or in elaborate combinations; they can be used for pure decoration or, in the case of sailing, for some very practical purposes.

Many decorative knots have long nautical traditions and seamen and sailors, particularly those who served aboard the great sailing vessels of the eighteenth and nineteen centuries, developed decorative knot tying into a folk art.

Lanyard Knot

A lanyard is usually worn around the the neck or attached to a belt for the purpose of holding a wide variety of objects – from knives and whistles to watches and binoculars. Lanyards have a long nautical history and, because the cord is left in view, sailors often decorated them with a range of elaborate knots. The knife lanyard knot is one of the most attractive and subsequently one of the most widely used. At first sight it may appear difficult to tie, but be patient, follow the step-by-step instructions, 'work' the knot into its final form, and you will be rewarded with a beautiful and functional decorative knot.

It may help to create the first two steps of the knot around your hand, with this pattern on the front and the main loop running behind your hand.

③ ④ ⑤

Monkey's Fist

The monkey's fist is a decorative knot that also has many practical uses, the most common being the knot at the end of a heaving line. To give the monkey's fist more weight, it is often tied over a spherical object such as a heavy ball or stone. Smaller knots can be tied over golf balls; if the line is required to float, use a rubber ball. Decoratively, it makes an attractive end to any cord, and is regularly used at the end of pull cords.

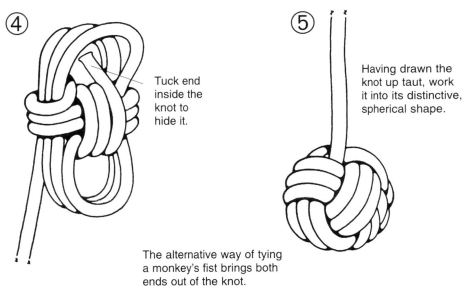

④ Tuck end
inside the
knot to
hide it.

⑤ Having drawn the
knot up taut, work
it into its distinctive,
spherical shape.

The alternative way of tying
a monkey's fist brings both
ends out of the knot.

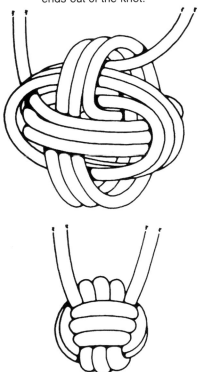

Turk's Head

Turk's head knots have long been recognised for their highly decorative attributes. Leonardo da Vinci drew them in the fifteenth century and they are still widely used today. They are usually tied around cylindrical objects – in most cases as pure decoration (for example, to decorate a tiller). But they can also serve many practical sailing purposes, and are often used to mark the rudder's

amidships position on a ship's wheel.

There are many recorded variations of these knots. The Turk's head shown here – a single-strand, four-lead, three-bight version – is one of the most popular. To create the finished compact knot as in step 6, the slack will need to be worked out. This is done gradually, by starting at one end of the cord and progressing through the knot to the other end. It may also help to use a pair of thin-nosed pliers.

① Create the first step of this knot around your hand with this pattern on the front and the main loop running behind your hand.

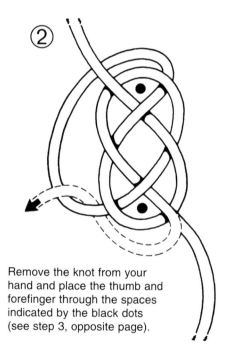

② Remove the knot from your hand and place the thumb and forefinger through the spaces indicated by the black dots (see step 3, opposite page).

④ Place the loosely formed knot around a cylindrical object.

⑤ Tuck the second lead next to the first lead, as shown here, and follow around as many times as desired.

Turk's Head – Flat Form

This method shows how to tie a Turk's head in a flat form. The knot can be left in this form to create, for example, a mat or decorative fender. Alternatively, it can be turned down and worked over a cylindrical object to form a decorative covering.

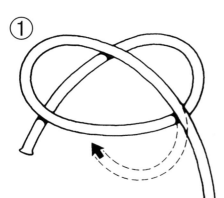

To tie the knot in its flat form, work on a flat surface and take out the slack while threading through the second lead to keep the knot tight and compact.

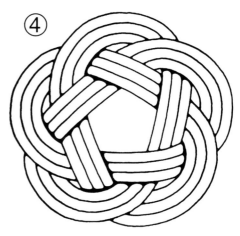

The first lead can be followed around by the second lead as many times as required to create the finished knot. Always keep the second lead on the same side as the first lead (the lead that created the pattern) and tuck the ends in neatly to hide them.

Flat Sennet

Sennets are one or more intertwined strands that can be tied from a wide variety of materials. They have a vast range of decorative applications, but also have many practical advantages. In the past sailors exploited the excellent 'cling' and surface-wear qualities of 'sennet lines.'

This simple, three-strand, plait or braid sennet is also know as the English or common sennet. Arrange the three strands as in step 1 and, if necessary, secure them in a straight line with a clip or clamp. To achieve a neat, compact sennet as in step 6, tighten and arrange the plait at each step of tying. Sennets can be finished off in a variety of ways, depending on their final use. The simplest method is by clamping or seizing with thin string and then trimming off the excess.

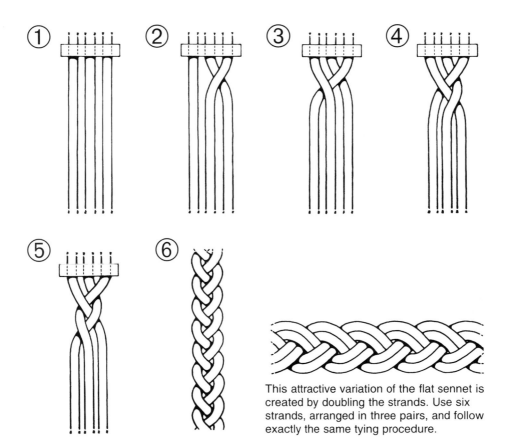

This attractive variation of the flat sennet is created by doubling the strands. Use six strands, arranged in three pairs, and follow exactly the same tying procedure.

Ocean Plait

This classic flat knot is found all over the world in a surprising number of situations but its use as a mat or tread on board a ship or boat is one of its common and practical uses.

The size of the example shown here, which is one of the most widely used, is based on three side bights.

The pattern can be made more solid by increasing the number of times the lead is followed around, but the actual size of the knot cannot be increased. To increase the size of the knot, the number of bights has to be increased. For example, make six or nine bights to create a long, narrow ocean plait for a companionway on board a ship or boat.

Once the pattern has been established with the three side bights, the knot can be doubled by following the pattern around with one of the ends.

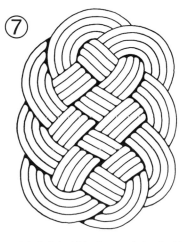

The knot can be doubled or followed around as many times as desired. It can also be left loosely formed as shown above, or it can be tightened and made solid, as in step 7.

To finish, hide the ends by tucking them into the weave on the underside of the knot. If the knot is to be used as a mat, the whole structure can be greatly stengthened by sewing together all of the intersecting points with strong thread.

87

9

Net Making

Nets can be tied in a variety of sizes
for many different uses, from fishing
to storage, and it is always useful to
be able to construct your own
custom-sized net. One of the most
popular, and important, sailing uses
is safety netting between guard-rails
and deck. This does not only prevent
people, especially small children,
from falling overboard, but it also
prevents the loss of important
equipment that can often prove
impossible to recover.

To construct a net you will require
a reel of good netting twine, a net
needle and a piece of wood with
straight edges.

A net needle will make it easy to thread the twine and will save you from having to pull the whole line through at each turn.

A wooden straightedge will enable you to hold and check the mesh to give a uniform pattern.

Side rope or guard-rail

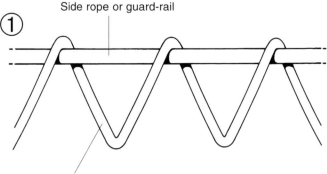

Looped netting twine. For additional strength the twine can be secured to the side rope or guard-rail by using a clove hitch at each apex.

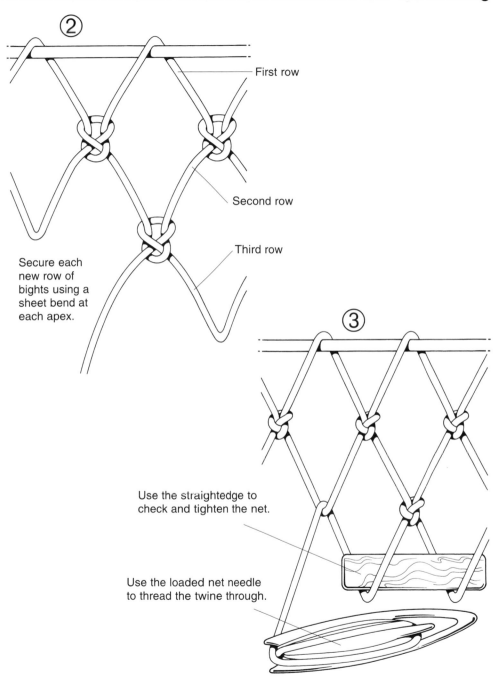

② First row

Second row

Third row

Secure each
new row of
bights using a
sheet bend at
each apex.

③

Use the straightedge to
check and tighten the net.

Use the loaded net needle
to thread the twine through.

Glossary

Astern At or toward the rear part of a boat or the reversing manoeuvre of a vessel, as in: *full speed astern!*

Belay To secure a rope or line with figure-of-eight turns around a cleat.

Bend The action of tying two ropes together by their ends. Also, the name given to the group of knots used to tie lines to each other or to some other object.

Bight The slack section of the rope between the working end and the standing end. The term is particularly used when this section of the rope is formed into a loop or turned back on itself. Knots tied 'in the bight' or 'on the bight' do not use the ends in the tying process.

Bollard A large fixed post made of iron or wood to which a boat is moored.

Bow The front end of a boat.

Braid To interweave several strands.

Breaking strength, strain or load The manufacturer's estimate of the load that will cause a rope to part. This calculation is based on the strength of a dry line under steady pull; it generally takes no account of wetness, wear and tear, knots or shock loading. Lines are weaker when wet, worn or knotted, and the manufacturer's estimate cannot be regarded as a safe working load.

Cable A heavy fibre or wire rope or chain of large diameter; anchor warp or chain.

Cable-laid Rope formed of three right-handed hawsers laid up left-handed to make a larger, nine-strand rope or cable.

Chafe To make or become worn or frayed by rubbing.

Cleat A wood or metal T-shaped fitting around which a rope or line is wound to be secured.

Cord Several tightly twisted yarns making a line with a diameter of less than half an inch.

Cordage Collective name for ropes and cords; especially used to describe the ropes in a ship's rigging.

Core The inner or central part found in ropes and sennets of more than three strands, and in most braided lines. Formed from a bundle of parallel strands or loosely twisted yarn running the length of the rope. Also the central part of a monkey's fist knot, inserted to add weight.

Eye Loop formed at the end of a length of rope.

Fender A cushion of flexible material positioned on the sides of a boat to prevent damage when tied alongside a dock or another boat.

Fid Tapered wooden pin used to work or loosen strands of rope.

Fray To unravel, especially the end of a piece of rope.

Heaving line A line, with a weighted knot tied at one end, that is attached to another heavier line and is thrown from boat to shore or to another vessel. The purpose of the line is to draw behind it a heavier line that will be used for tying up or mooring.

Grommet A ring, usually made of metal or twisted rope; also a small eyelet in a sail.

Hawser A rope or cable, five to

24ins in circumference, large enough for towing or mooring.

Hitch Knot made to secure a rope to a ring, spar, etc, or to another rope.

Lanyard A short length of rope or cord made decorative with knots and sennets. Used to secure personal objects; usually worn around the neck or attached to a belt.

Lay The direction, right- or left-handed, of the twist in the strands that form a rope.

Line Generic name for cordage with no specific purpose, although it can describe a particular use (clothes-line, fishing line, etc).

Loop Part of a rope that is bent so that it comes together across itself.

Make fast To secure a rope or line to a cleat, etc.

Nip The binding pressure within a knot that stops it from slipping.

Plain-laid rope Three-stranded rope laid (twisted) to the right.

Plait Pronounced *plat*. To intertwine strands in a pattern.

Port The left-hand side of a boat looking forward.

Reeve The act of threading or passing a rope through an aperture such as a ring, or block.

Running rigging Adjustable rope or wire used to control the sails.

Seizing To bind two ropes or cords together.

Sennet Braided cordage (flat, round or square), formed from three to nine cords.

Small stuff Thin cordage, twine, string, rope or line that has a circumference of less than 1in, or a diameter of less than $\frac{1}{2}$in.

Spar A mast, boom, gaff or sprit.

Splice A join in rope or wire created by tucking the rope's strands into its own lay; to join the ends of rope by interweaving its strands.

Standing end The end of the standing part of the rope.

Standing part The part of the rope that is fixed and under tension (as opposed to the free working end with which the knot is tied).

Starboard The right-hand side of a boat looking forward.

Stern The back of a boat.

Stopper knot Any terminal knot used to prevent it passing back through a fitting such as a block or fairlead; or to bind the end of a line, cord or rope to prevent it from unravelling; also used to provide a decorative end.

Strand Yarns twisted together in the opposite direction to the yarn itself. Rope made from strands (rope that is not braided) is called laid line.

Taut Tightly stretched.

Thimble A metal or plastic eye used to shape an eye splice and prevent chafe.

Twine Thin line of various types for various uses, as in whipping twine, etc.

Warp A general term for mooring ropes, anchor cable, etc.

Whipping Tightly wrapping small stuff around the end of a cord or rope to prevent it from fraying.

Work To draw and shape a knot; to make the final arrangement.

Working end The part of the rope or cord actively used in tying a knot. The opposite of the standing end.

Yarn The basic element of rope or cord formed from artificial or synthetic filaments or natural fibres.

Index of Knots

Anchor Bend, 71

Back Splice, 32
Bends, 43
Bowline, 55
Bowline, running, 56
Bowline, Spanish, 60
Bowline on the Bight, 57
Bowline – Attaching to a ring, 58
Buntline Hitch, 72

Carrick Bend, 46
Cat's Paw, 75
Cleating a line, 17
Clove Hitch, 66
Common Whipping, 22
Constrictor Knot, 68

Decorative Knots, 77
Double Fisherman's Knot, 50
Doughnut, 42

Eye Splice, 34
Eye Splice with Thimble, 35

Figure-of-Eight, 39
Figure-of-Eight Bend, 51
Figure-of-Eight Loop, 54
Fisherman's Bend, 71
Fisherman's Knot, 49
Fisherman's Knot, double, 50
Flat Seizing, 28
Flat Sennet, 85

Half Hitches, 64
Heaving Line Knot, 41
Hitches, 63

Lanyard Knot, 78
Loops, 53

Monkey's Fist, 80
Multiple Overhand Knot, 40

Net Making, 89

Ocean Plait, 86
Overhand Knot, 38

Palm-and-Needle Seizing, 29
Palm-and-Needle Whipping, 23
Pile Hitch, 70

Racking Seizing, 30
Reef Knot, 44
Rigger's Bend, 47
Rolling Hitch, 73
Rope Ends, 21
Round Turn and Two Half Hitches, 65
Running Bowline, 56

Sealing Ends, 25
Sennet, 85
Seizings, 27
Seizing, Palm-and-Needle, 29
Sheepshank, 15
Sheet Bend, 45
Short Splice, 33
Snaked Whipping, 24
Spanish Bowline, 60
Splicings, 31
Stopper Knot, 41
Stopper Knots, 37
Surgeon's Knot, 48

Three-Part Crown, 59
Transom Knot, 69
Turk's Head, 82
Turk's Head – Flat Form, 84

Waggoner's Hitch, 74
Whipping, 22
Whipping, Snaked, 24
Whipping, Palm-and-Neddle, 23